Touch t

About Lesser-Known People
in the Bible

by
Louis G. Miller, C.SS.R.

Liguori Publications
One Liguori Drive
Liguori, Missouri 63057

To my sister,
a Redemptoristine Cloistered Nun,
truly touched by Christ.

Imprimi Potest:
Edmund T. Langton, C.SS.R.
Provincial, St. Louis Province
Redemptorist Fathers
September 2, 1977

Imprimatur:
St. Louis, September 7, 1977
+John N. Wurm
Vicar General of St. Louis

ISBN 0-89243-072-9
Copyright © 1978, Liguori Publications

Printed in U.S.A.

Library of Congress Catalog Card Number: 77-90929

Photo Credits

Cover photo by Ewing Galloway

Ricarda Schwerin: 9, 23, 37, 52, 60, 80.
Norman Muckerman, C.SS.R. 16, 87.
Ewing Galloway 30, 67, 74.
Burton Holmes from Ewing Galloway: 45.

TABLE OF CONTENTS

INTRODUCTION

Scattered through the Gospels and Acts of the Apostles are incidents involving people without names, or, if they have names, not much more is known beyond that. I have always been intrigued by these passing references, and have wanted to know more about the people involved. But since in the historical record there is no data, beyond fragmentary details, that can help us fill out the picture as to what they were really like, this is an attempt to let imagination serve that purpose.

The circumstances in which these individuals are mentioned give us at least a clue as to what kind of personality they possessed. Is it stretching reality, for instance, to see an active, outspoken personality in the Syro-Phoenician woman who responded so boldly to our Lord when he at first refused to help her because she was a Gentile: "Even the dogs eat the crumbs."

As for Zebedee, the father of James and John, how did he feel when his two sons, at the call of Christ, abruptly left him there on the shore of the Sea of Galilee, without a backward glance? I think it is not unrealistic to suppose that he felt like many a parent today who has great plans for a son or daughter, and sees that boy or girl take up a way of life entirely different than had been anticipated.

Or consider the twin of Thomas the apostle; I have to suppose that he had the same opportunities as Thomas to listen to Christ. Not hearing the same call that Thomas heard, he must have been somewhat puzzled by the unfolding of events, and regretful that he had missed out on something important.

Ten of the people in this book are from the Gospels. Two, Joseph Barsabbas and Lydia, are from the Acts of the Apostles. Lydia is especially significant, because she was a chief instrument in the founding of St. Paul's first Christian community in Europe.

I hope Lydia and all these others will forgive me if I have taken liberties and drawn conclusions which might surprise them, even in their present blessed state. I have tried sincerely not to do violence to the Scriptures, even when I allowed my imagination to build on sparse details.

1

The Woman Who Contradicted Christ

(Saving Faith)

A woman, whose little daughter
had an unclean spirit,
came in and fell down at his feet.
She was a Gentile,
a Syro-Phoenician by birth.
And she besought him
to cast the devil out of her daughter.
But he said to her,
"Let the children first have their fill,
for it is not fair to take the children's bread
and to cast it to the dogs."
But she answered and said to him,
"Yes, Lord; for even the dogs under the table
eat of the children's crumbs."
And he said to her,
"Because of this answer, go thy way;
the devil has gone out of thy daughter."

Mark 7:25-29

An ancient well in the Holy Land

They don't push me around,
I say what I think.
They don't expect a woman to speak up,
these Jews around me;
their women hide behind their shawls,
they don't dare speak their minds.
I know their ways,
these Jews who live in Tyre.
We meet and gossip at the village well.
A Gentile like myself is second class;
they think they are the chosen race,
perhaps they are.
I find myself attracted to their God,
not to my native gods of Tyre and Sidon,

strange, misshapen gods.
Yahweh of the Jews makes sense to me;
he loves his people
and rewards their love.
It's only that his people are so prickly;
I wish they weren't so arrogant about it.
If Yahweh called them to his special love,
am I to be excluded from his love?
I don't believe it
and I tell them so.

I never was a person to stay quiet.
My husband always was the quiet one;
I loved him for it.
But now and then
I lost my patience with him.
He was content to let things as they were.
"You're only causing trouble,"
he would say.
"You're not a Jew and never can you be;
the best thing you can do is be content
and let the Jews alone."
Then I would say,
"But what if Yahweh is the only god?"

Our only child lay ill upon her bed
with a strange illness, foam upon her lips
and hatred in her eyes; our ten year old
who always had been so affectionate,
strange, terrible sounds she uttered in her sleep.
Her fever rose, she trembled violently
and shook the bed;
my heart was torn with grief.
The doctors wagged their solemn heads and

sighed and said,
"The case is one beyond our skill."
I scolded them,
"Healing is your business,
what is wrong?
Why can't you mix some herbs and
    cure my child?"
We saw our little Dorcas gasp for breath
and I grew frantic;
where could I turn for help?
And then I heard
a holy man named Jesus was close by.
They said he often prayed and cured the sick,
and even raised a little girl to life
and gave her to her parents.
"Go out and find this man,"
I told my husband,
"and tell him that our daughter is so ill."
He would not go.
"This Jesus is a Jew," he said to me,
"and we are Gentiles.
You know what that means.
If he works wonders,
he will not do his wonderworking here."
But I was angry
and I told him so.

I hurried from the house and through the streets,
asking all those I met about the Christ.
And then I saw a crowd before a house
and knew he must be there.
I could not wait,
but hurried to him, pushing through the throng
which pressed him close.

I had no fear or shame.
The tears sprang to my eyes,
I clasped his feet,
"Have pity, Lord," I said,
"have pity on my daughter who is ill
and close to death.
Some say she is possessed.
I cannot bear the thought,
I cannot bear it, Lord,
have pity!"
I felt his eyes upon me, but his words
seemed cruel:
"I cannot help your child,
I am a Jew;
my people must come first, the bread
must first be given to my own,
and not to the dogs outside."
I think that he was testing me, but still
I felt my anger rise,
"Nay, Lord," I said;
"we may be dogs,
but still deserve the crumbs."
I dared not lift my eyes,
but felt his hand
upon my head
and heard his voice,
"Daughter," is what he said,
"your soul is open to the saving truth;
go home in peace,
your faith has saved your child."
And then my heart was suddenly at peace.
I knew his words were true,
but more than that,
I knew that he was Lord and Master of us all,

and loved me as he loved his chosen Jews.

Some twenty years have passed.
My daughter, grown,
now holds a little daughter of her own,
and we are Christians, all, my husband too;
for Philip came and told us of the Lord.
We hope to live and die within this faith.
If any challenge me, I tell them so;
I have not lost my tongue.
They know me well,
I'm not afraid to say what's on my mind.
They tell me women should defer to men.
I try to do so, but the Lord knows well
I sometimes fail; men can be so stupid.
But what I ask for is to love the truth
and to love Christ,
my way, my truth, my life.

2

Zebedee: What's a Father to Do?

(God's Call)

As he was walking along the Sea of Galilee, he caught sight of two other brothers, James, Zebedee's son, and his brother John. They too were in their boat, getting their nets in order with their father. He called them, and immediately they abandoned boat and father to follow him.

Matthew 4:18-22

Lake Gennesaret

I don't know what got into James and John,
but does a father ever know his sons?
He hopes that they will follow in his steps;
they seem to like him and admire his ways.
Then suddenly the moment of surprise —
they turn their backs on all he had supposed
would be their choice.
What can a father do?
What could I do that day
   they broke my heart . . .?

Fishing in Lake Gennesaret was my life;
I never wanted anything but this.
I loved the quiet of the early dawn,

and then the gradual jostle of the men
coiling their nets and pushing off from shore
in several boats. My friends and neighbors, these,
Andrew of course and Simon,
  with his blustering ways.
We knew each other well, and I was proud
my two strong sons were with me on my boat.
And when, with strain and sweat we cast the net,
then saw it sink, and watched with anxious eyes,
and shouted at each other in our joy
to find it filled with shining, squirming fish
ready for market at Capernaum,
how peaceful then to rest our tired arms
and know that we were one in mind and heart.
The future seemed secure, no clouds at all.

Then Jesus came one day,
and stood and watched,
as on the shore we worked at mending nets.
I paid no heed: another holy man!
They praised his preaching —
  he could draw a crowd.
But so could others who had gone before
and faded out; I had no time to listen.
But John and James, I never thought to see it,
were swept away.
"Come follow me," he said — no more than that.
He waited quietly.
They stood there by the nets and looked at me
as if to say, "We hope you understand;
there is no other way for us to go."
And off they went without another word.
I saw them walk with him along the shore

and never felt so empty and alone.
"Dreamers!"
is what I wanted to cry out.
"Your holy man will lead you into jail
like Theodas, who died a year ago
gasping and screaming on a Roman cross."
But something made me simply stand and stare.
I'm not a pious man, but I fear God.
His workings are beyond me, that's for sure;
but my two sons, it seems, had heard his voice.

My wife Salome would not let me rest.
"Our sons," she said, "why did you let them go?
And who does this man Jesus think he is
to steal our sons away?"
I finally said:
"He's more than just an ordinary man;
there's something in his eyes. . . ."
At that my wife
began to dream, as women will. "Suppose
he is Elias come to life again.
The Scriptures tell us that he will return
triumphant. Think what it would mean
to have our sons beside him in his triumph."
I could not stop her foolish fantasy;
she was ambitious, this good wife of mine.
"You must be sure to ask where they have gone,
and I will search out Jesus,
and tell him John and James are fine young men
who can be counted on to do God's work,
and he should put them on his right and left
on that day when he shows
    the power of God. . . ."

For thirty years the memories have stayed bright,
and now we sit, an old man and his wife,
at sunset near the Sea of Galilee,
and think of happier days that we have known.
The younger men must do the fishing now;
we have long hours in which to sit and think
of what has happened,
  and what might have been.
Our James is dead, killed in Jerusalem
because he was a follower of Christ
and dared proclaim it to the Sanhedrin.
He was a child of thunder, Jesus said,
and thundering out against the Pharisees
as leader of the followers of Christ
meant savage death in cruel Jerusalem.
John was our strange one,
wanting to be alone,
looking across the water in a trance.
And yet his softness had a little steel.
We heard that he alone, of all the twelve,
with Mary and some other women too,
stood by the Cross of Jesus till the end
and had his body laid within the tomb.

One visit more we had from John our son
when he and Simon came to Galilee
with Andrew and the others, Matthew, too,
and asked if they could use my boat to fish.
I was not with them, but I later heard
that Jesus had appeared to them at dawn
beside the lake, and told them, "Feed my sheep."
I talked to John, and he would only say,
"Matthew will tell you all you need to know."

A tax collector, one of Jesus' twelve!
Now that was hard for me to understand!
But John said Matthew was an honest man
and best remembered all the words of Christ.
And so John left; we have not seen him since.
He said that he must travel to lands afar
to tell of Christ.
In these, our later years,
my wife and I have come to know him too
through Matthew's preaching in Capernaum —
that Christ had died,
but rose and will return.
We count ourselves among his followers.

We do have faith, and yet we mourn for James.
A young man still,
why did he die so young?
And why must John serve God so far away?
But still we are content, and are at peace.
God will provide, and in his own good time
we hope to see his face,
and see our sons.

The Man No Chains Could Bind

(Power of Jesus' Name)

*They came to Gerasene territory on the
other side of the lake. As he got out of
the boat, he was immediately met by a man
from the tombs who had an unclean spirit.
The man had taken refuge among the tombs;
he could no longer be restrained even with
a chain. In fact he had frequently been
secured with handcuffs and chains, but had
pulled the chains apart and smashed the
fetters. Uninterruptedly night and day, amid
the tombs and on the hillsides, he screamed and
gashed himself with stones. Catching sight
of Jesus at a distance, he ran up and did
him homage, shrieking in a loud voice, "Why
meddle with me, Jesus, Son of God Most High?
I implore you in God's name do not torture
me." Jesus had been saying to him, "Unclean
spirit, come out of the man!"*

     Mark 5:1-8

A rock tomb in the Kidron Valley

Elymas is my name,
the land of the Gerasenes my home,
Decapolis they call it,
east of the Sea of Galilee.
Old now and decrepit,
I must depend on others for my strength.
There was a time,
forty years ago,
when people feared my strength,
for it could bruise their heads
and break their bones.
God made me huge in size —
"Elymas our red-haired giant,"
they used to say,

"can carry five men under either arm."
But I was a gentle giant
and never one to brawl.

Then suddenly my life began to change.
Something within me, or someone,
rose up in wrath.
It was as if I watched him from afar.
I could not hold him;
they said I was possessed.
An evil spirit, nay, a legion of them,
their voices jangling in their quarreling,
had mastered me and held me in their bond.
I raged and roared.
The townsfolk shunned me like a dog gone mad;
my sisters fled and hid at my approach.
I snarled and showed my teeth at them.
One day
five strong men came
 and threw me to the ground
and bound me tight
 with chains on hands and feet.
They thought I was secure.
I played the game
until it suited me to show my strength.
My demons rose and laughed derisively
and broke the chains
as if they were of wax.
Then, foaming at the mouth I rushed at those
strong men who tried to put me in restraint.
They scattered, but a few of them I caught
and smashed their faces,
jeering at their screams.

I did not want to hurt them in this way.
These were my townsfolk,
the people that I loved;
but in my soul
the prince of hatred ruled,
and violence is the bread of life to him.

The demons let me see what I had done
and what I had become.
They jeered at me.
And in my sadness, to the tombs I ran
and stripped my clothing.
Naked I stood in view,
and gashed myself with stones until I bled,
and clawed the ground and vomited my filth.
To passerby I wanted to cry,
"Help!"

The demons would not let me say the word,
but from my lips, unbidden, there poured forth
a putrid river of obscenity,
for these were unclean spirits who haunted me.
Why had they come?
If God is good, why did they torture me?
I was a sinner, but no worse than most.
Why was God silent, he who made the world?
Why did he let the demons work their will?

There was no answer until Jesus came.
I did not know him then,
but some great power
above the power of hell that roared in me
drove me from out the tombs at his approach.

I ran across the fields,
fell at his feet,
and mouthed the dust in my abject despair.
The demons shrieked:
"Leave us alone and go your way,
you holy one, or you will pay;
leave us alone or you will pay."
But Jesus did not flinch.
He looked at me,
or at the evil spirits that were within me,
and said:
"Go out of him,
you unclean spirit!"
His words were a command,
the demons fled.
I lay there in the dust
and could not rise
until he stooped and gently took my arm.
And then I stood
in joy and peace,
for I had seen
the power of God
and never would
the demons come
to rage within
this Gerasene again.

With all my heart I longed to die for him.
"Please let me follow you,"
I blurted out;
but he replied:
"You have another task.
Tell all who live here in Decapolis

that God remains the ruler of the world,
and he has sent his Son
to save mankind."
And that has been my mission all these years,
to speak of Christ and all his wondrous works.
For Peter came to all our towns and preached.
And Mark was with him — a scribe
who wrote about the things he saw and heard,
and saw and wrote about the setting free
of this poor Gerasene, the gentle giant
who knows there is not any power on earth
or over it,
or under it as well,
so great as is the power of Jesus' name.
And in that name
I hope to live and die.

4

The Boy With Five Barley Loaves

(Charity in Action)

One of Jesus' disciples, Andrew,
Simon Peter's brother,
remarked to him:
"There is a lad here
who has five barley loaves
and a couple of dried fish,
but what good is that for so many?"

John 6:8

Mt. Tabor, the place of Christ's Transfiguration

Nicholaus is my name,
a deacon in good repute.
At twelve years of age
I had a grownup's job.
I had my mother to take care of
after my father's death.
There wasn't much time for play
with other boys my age.
I was always on the lookout
for money to buy our bread.
We were very poor,
just the two of us;
we struggled to stay alive.

I saw a crowd one day
churning dust upon the road.
Many from our village
went out into the hill country
to hear a holy man preach.
"They will be looking for food,"
I said to myself.
"If only I could get hold
of a few dozen loaves."
It wasn't very likely.
I had no money to buy bread.
My mother said to me:
"Let us follow the crowd."
We took our last two loaves,
I begged some bread from an aunt
who lived next door —
she always liked me —
and she gave me three loaves
and added two dried fish.
I put the food in a basket
and we followed the people
out into the hills.
That's when I first saw Jesus.
He was standing quietly
under a tree,
watching the people
as they gathered around him.
I got as close to him as I could;
something about him held me,
I don't know what it was,
something in his eyes . . . .
He looked at me and smiled.
I said in my heart:

"This is the man I must follow."
We were there all that day
and the crowd continued to grow —
more than a thousand of them —
the largest crowd I ever saw.
We forgot all about eating
while he spoke to us.
He didn't seem to shout,
yet everybody was able to hear him.
There was no stirring in the crowd,
even when he paused and rested.
Everybody sat there thinking
or talking quietly to each other.
Before we knew it, it was evening.
I heard Jesus say
to some who were his helpers,
"Where can we find food
to feed this crowd?"
But no one had brought anything.
I was standing close by.
A man named Andrew —
I heard them call him by that name —
looked at my basket and said:
"Here is a boy
with a few loaves and fish,
but that won't go very far."
Jesus took my basket —
I didn't even think
of asking any money for it —
and I saw him bless it.
Then suddenly the basket
was filled to the very top.

Andrew and some others
began to hand out the loaves;
and as fast as they emptied it,
the basket seemed to fill up again,
and the same with the fish.
I didn't know what to make of it.
After they all had finished eating,
there was still enough left
to fill my basket and ten others.

My mother didn't know what to say;
I never saw her like that.
Some of the men came to Jesus.
I heard them say to him:
"Master, be our leader,
be our conquering king."
But Jesus looked sad,
as if they didn't understand,
and he walked off by himself
down the hill toward the lake.
But before he departed
he smiled at me standing there
and put his hand on my head.
Then he took my hand
and put two shekels into it
(one of his helpers
had the money in a purse),
and he said to me:
"This is for the bread and the fish
that you provided for our meal."
I didn't know what to say;
I stood there speechless,
and so did my mother.

We watched him walk away,
but I said to myself:
"I will follow him until death."

Now I am old,
my mother is dead.
I have kept my word;
I followed him to Jerusalem,
and saw him die on a cross.
I never gave up hope,
and when Andrew told me
he had risen from the grave,
I knew it had to be.
I've never been a dreamer;
I'm a practical man.
They made me a deacon
here in Capernaum
to help with the serving,
to look after the needy.
All these years I have labored;
they know they can count on me.
I don't have any visions,
I have to be active;
I'm glad to be active
for Jesus my Savior.

5

Lazarus:
I Was Dead
and Now
I Am Alive

(Belief in the Resurrection)

Jesus cried out with a loud voice,
"Lazarus, come forth!"
And at once he who had been
dead came forth, bound
feet and hands with bandages,
and his face was tied up with
a cloth.

John 11:44

A rock tomb, much like the one Lazarus was buried in

Twelve years ago I died.
They wrapped my body in the funeral shroud
and placed it in the tomb.
Then suddenly
in that dark silence
my name was spoken.
It was as if
something within me was waiting for that word.
There was light in the darkness,
warmth in the grave's chill,
and I stood up
with a surge of new life
and came out of the tomb,
responding to Christ's call.

Regretting and rejoicing are in conflict;
they color all my memories of that day.

I remember well my sickness,
my anxious sisters ever at my side,
the doctor's grave and solemn look,
the fever's rage
and then the shuddering chills.
But at the end I felt no pain at all,
only weakness down to my fingertips,
and a great unconcern
about life or death
or what might happen after.
I saw, as a sailor sees, a shrouded land
in the early morning mist
and longed with all my heart to make for it.
I knew, as I had never known before,
a peace that filled the spaces of my heart.
And so my small boat grated on the shore.
I waited, longing for what lay beyond,
not knowing why it was I had to wait,
until the day when Jesus spoke my name
and roused me from my sleep
within the tomb.

I had been part of the crowd one summer day
within a shady Temple portico
when Jesus spoke.
"If any man thirst," he said,
"let him come, and I will satisfy his thirst."
I thought his eye
caught my eye at that moment,
though others doubtless could have said the same.

But in that moment something passed between us
the loyalty of my heart,
and his grateful acceptance of my love.
We did not speak, we did not need to speak.
When I returned to Bethany that night,
thinking my own thoughts,
Martha had the basin for my washing;
she was always the practical one.
Mary liked to watch the evening sunset;
I heard her, near the doorway,
speaking to someone,
and there he was, Jesus.
He had followed me to our home
and asked us humbly
if he might stay and rest with us that night.
From his first words we had no other course
but love and loyalty with all our hearts.
When he was in Jerusalem thereafter
it was his custom
at the close of day
to come and spend the night with us at home.
In those peaceful and rewarding hours
it seemed that there his tension was relaxed.
And when my sister Martha scolded Mary
for being such a dreamer and forgetting
to set the table for our honored guest,
he smiled at her with fondness and he said
to all of us:
"Be patient with each other,
each has a gift to offer to the Lord
and every gift is precious;
yet I tell you
to seek and find the Lord is best of all."

But I could smell the storm wind in the city
and feel the hatred heavy in the air.
He whipped the merchants from the Temple court
and to the Pharisees he said in anger,
"You whitened sepulchers,
you prophet slayers!"
They had determined in their council meeting
that he must die;
there was no other option.

And so it was the day that I fell ill,
and he was far away from Bethany.
My sister sent a trusted friend to tell him,
but still he lingered
to the day I died.
When he came back —
 a hurried three-day journey —
he found me in my grave, my story ended.
Then with my weeping sisters and a crowd
of friends who gathered to console the two
(and there were present enemies as well),
he stood before the tomb and wept and groaned
(seeing the sorrows of humanity)
and cried out in an almighty voice,
"Lazarus,
come forth!"
I heard that voice
as one who hears a cry across the waters
in the still coolness of an early dawn.
It was a trumpet call that stirred my bones,
cascading through my tissues like fresh blood.
I could not possibly resist that summons.
The burial bonds I loosened from my feet;

I stood,
and walked with firmness toward the light,
hearing as in a daze the shouts and screams,
embraced by my sisters, sobbing in their joy,
and Christ withdrawn a little from the crowd.
They looked at him with awe,
but some with anger;
his love restored a dead man to this life,
and there were living men who died to truth
that day when Christ commanded,
"Come forth!"
and set the seal on all that he had said.

Ten years have brought their changes to my life.
Martha is dead; she worked beyond her strength
with deeds of charity for all the poor.
My younger sister chose another way,
a better choice, Christ called it, even though
Martha and Mary shared his equal love.
Those tranquil days in Bethany have passed
and all is turmoil.
In Jerusalem
the jails are filled with followers of Christ,
and not a few have died, as Stephen did,
beneath a hail of stones from vengeful hands.
I live in Antioch now, where just last week
we Christians, as they call us, summoned Paul
and Barnabas, and sent them out to preach
the word of Christ in near and distant towns.
I too one day may follow in their steps
and set my sail for some far distant shore,
perhaps as far as Gaul, to tell them there,
here is a man who once was dead and lives.

Christ raised me for the task, and he himself
was crucified and buried and arose,
for he is God, you must believe in him.

I dream of this, but oftener I dream
of hearing him a second time command:
"Lazarus, come forth!"
And this time I will stir myself and go
away from shadows
into light and peace.

6

The Other Twin: Brother to Thomas

(Doubt Removed)

Then Thomas
(the name means "twin")
said to his fellow disciples,
"Let us go along
to die with him."
John 11:16

The Church of the Nativity, Bethlehem

My twin brother was Thomas,
an early follower of Jesus.
Strange how the ways of brothers
can follow the same furrow
and suddenly diverge.
We were close in mind and heart,
as close as olives growing on a branch,
or so I was convinced.
But he had some hidden depth
I could not plumb.
A turn of phrase,
a sudden thought
would take me by surprise and puzzle me.
He had a way of questioning

that taxed my patience,
much as I loved him.
Thomas was too practical, I thought.
I was the dreamer;
he would scoff at me,
"When I see it, I'll believe it,"
was what he often said.

I was with him when he first met Christ.
There was a wedding feast at Cana;
the Mother of Christ was present with her Son
and some few friends,
more indeed than were expected,
but that's the way it is at celebrations.
Jesus impressed me,
I must honestly admit.
Outwardly he looked like any man
sweating and dusty in the summer heat.
But still you paused before the inner light
that somehow he projected.
Here at Cana the first of Jesus' wonders
came to pass.
I did not see it happen —
others told me.
There were some stone jars
  nearly filled with water
standing along the wall. Jesus said,
"Let it be wine!"
The steward was called in, and when he tasted,
he looked around, astounded, at us all.
Thomas said he saw it, and that moment
became convinced that Jesus was divine.
"Now this is truly marvelous," I said,

"my questioning brother won because of wine!"
But something happened to him there at Cana,
a choice and a decision that he made,
and I his twin could only stand and wonder.

Oh, I believed in God, as Thomas did;
and as for Christ,
I followed from afar,
wanting it both ways,
balancing God and comfort.
But there were those,
  and Thomas was among them,
who left their families and their friends behind
to seek ideals beyond all common sense,
ideals pregnant with the smell of death.
Caution kept me from this hopeless choice,
but still at times I envied my twin Thomas.
He was at peace, and I could find no peace,
but fretted over small and trivial things.

I saw him little in those later months,
and when I did, he seemed preoccupied,
tired and dusty from his wanderings.
He came at times into Capernaum,
which was our native village and our home.
Our relatives were there among the townsfolk;
they didn't quite know what to make of Christ.
"His father was a carpenter," they said,
"from Nazareth, that quiet little town —
who could accept a prophet from that place?"
Then Thomas would get angry and cry out:
"Why are you so stubborn?
You've seen his wonders in the city streets.

Are you so blind you cannot read the signs?"
And then his relatives, and I among them,
would be embarrassed, turn away our eyes.
Thomas grown fanatic, what a shame.
His Christ could hold a crowd,
no doubt of that,
but some things that he said were hard to take.
"Do good to those who hate you" —
that's a sample.
How could we live by such a foolish law?

So Thomas went his way and I, his twin,
grew prosperous
in my comfortable home.
I heard reports of him from time to time.
They said that Christ was in Jerusalem
creating trouble everywhere he went —
confronting Caiaphas in the Temple square,
and lashing out in anger at the merchants
who trafficked loudly in the Temple porch.
There was one morning more when Thomas came
and stopped to see me in Capernaum.
He seemed distressed.
A friend had died, he said,
Lazarus by name, whose home was Bethany.
And Christ had said:
"We must return at once!"
"They hate us there," my brother said to me;
"if we go back it will be certain death."
"Then why go back?" I said;
"it seems so foolish."
But Thomas had that stubborn look about him.
"If I must die with him,

why then, so be it."
I simply could not understand my brother.
We said goodbye, and knew it was the end.

So here I am, now in my later years,
my family grown,
my wife long since gone.
And Thomas my twin — so often in my thoughts
he stands before me;
where is Thomas now?
I seek out visitors from other towns
to ask them what they may have heard of him.
And they have strange accounts
   of wondrous things.
Christ died,
and then came back to life, they say.
But I'll believe it if someday I see it;
that's what my brother Thomas used to say.
But if someday my brother comes again
from India, where they say that he has gone,
and tells me what I hear of Christ is true,
I also will believe.
Enough for me
if doubting Thomas is no more in doubt,
but in his soul believes
that Christ is God.

7

Nicodemus: A Cautious Teacher in Israel

(Courage of Conviction)

*A certain Pharisee named
Nicodemus, a member of the
Jewish Sanhedrin, came to
him at night. "Rabbi," he said,
"we know that you are a teacher
come from God, for no man can
perform signs and wonders such
as you perform unless God is
with him."*

John 3:1-2

Steps leading to the Tomb of Kings

What should I have done?
Could I have changed things
if I had shown more courage and more strength?
These are the questions that I ask myself,
I, Nicodemus,
member of the Sanhedrin,
respected teacher of God's chosen people.
This is what Jesus called me, I remember;
"You are a teacher,
and should read the signs," he said.
"How can the others see if you are blind?"
I saw,
and yet I did not want to see.
Men of learning can be cowards too,

and I was one.
I was afraid of what my friends would say,
my learned colleagues
with their pitying smiles.
A Pharisee, I smarted like the rest
when Jesus called us whitened sepulchers,
and said we put the load on other backs
and split the law,
and let ourselves go free.
"Hypocrites," he called us, and I sensed
the hatred that my learned colleagues felt.
But something in me answered to his challenge.
I knew that he was right
and felt ashamed,
and then and there resolved to test him out.

Why must I do everything in secret?
It was in secret that I sought him out,
and asked about his way.
I came at night
when no one was around.
He puzzled me, and yet I was attracted.
I heard him preaching in the Temple porch,
and what he said cut through my native caution.
I couldn't explain it,
but my heart was drawn;
and yet I came in secret, to my shame.
He listened to my questioning with kindness,
and then he said,
"You must be born again."
This puzzled me, but then he gently chided:
"You're a teacher;
the prophets clearly wrote about this day."

He took my hand
and looked at me with fondness.
"You must be open to the truth,"
he said,
"and not let caution keep the portals closed."
But that's my trouble, always asking questions,
afraid of answers,
afraid to take a stand.

I stood up in the meeting of the Council
discussing what to do.
It had been stated
a dead man, Lazarus, was once more living,
and Jesus had restored the man to life,
and crowds were thronging out
  to see the wonder.
"This Jesus threatens the established order,"
said Caiaphas, and nearly all agreed.
But I objected,
and for once showed spirit:
"Violence is not the way we should go.
Suppose the holy one we have been seeking
has truly come among us,
then in truth,
we must be open to the truth he brings."
And Joseph spoke, he of Arimathea,
and took my side;
but with what awful fury
they turned on us with anger and with scorn.
And Caiaphas,
      an I never trusted,
    d, in that cold and cruel way he had,
    his man must die!"

We left the Council chamber, Joseph and I,
shunned by all the rest.

And so the end drew near.
We were not summoned
the night they sent the guard to capture Christ
and brought him first to Annas,
then to Caiaphas.
He could expect no justice in that court.
I followed
as they brought him out to Pilate
and saw what Pilate's soldiers had achieved —
torn by the scourges,
thorns upon his head,
dressed like a mock king
with a reed as scepter.
I heard the cynical, sardonic Pilate,
standing beside his prisoner, say,
"Behold your king!"
He knew this would grate on Jewish ears.

And so I followed to the hill of Calvary,
and watched the drama to its bloody end.
I heard him cry out in his desolation,
and saw him die,
and thought the world would end.
But in the crashing thunder of that hour —
the shaking earth, the darkness of the sky —
this cautious Nicodemus
found his courage.
I knew what I must do, and found his Mother,
with Magdalene, and some other women too
and John.

A soldier helped us find some ladders —
Longinus was his name.
He humbly told us
that when Jesus cried out,
"My spirit I commend into your hands,"
he sensed a flood of light within his soul,
and knew that truly this was God's own Son.

And Joseph said that he would go to Pilate.
The Romans had a law —
a criminal's body
must be disposed of in a common grave.
And this is what they would have done
  with Jesus,
if Joseph had not gone,
a man of courage,
to Pilate, who had to hear him for his honor.
"If Christ is dead, my task is finished;
dispose of what is left as you see fit,"
were Pilate's words.

We gently pulled the nails from hands and feet,
took his blood-drained body from the cross,
placed it in his Mother's arms beneath,
and joined with grieving silence in her grief.
But then the time was short before the Sabbath;
we had to do our task while it was day.
My servant came with spices for embalming,
and Joseph led us to a new-hewn tomb.
It was his own that he had just prepared,
but now it was the Lord's.
Even in dying,
Jesus had no place to call his own.

We left him there at rest.
You know the sequel:
on Easter morning Jesus rose again
and turned our sorrow into peace and joy.
This cautious Nicodemus — praised be God! —
no longer seeks the Lord in darkened streets
and secretly, but speaks his holy name
in sunlight and wherever hearts are found
open to receive his saving grace.

Malchus: Sword in a Garden

(A Servant's Prayer)

But when they who were about
saw what would follow, they
said to him, "Lord, shall we
strike with the sword?" And
one of them struck the servant
of the high priest and cut
off his right ear. But Jesus
answered and said, "Bear with
them thus far." And he
touched his ear and healed him.

Luke 22:49-51

The name of the slave was
Malchus.

John 18:10

Olive trees near Gethsemane

It doesn't make sense:
that dark strange hour
under the olive trees
thirty years ago
stays in my memory.
Why can't I forget it?
The blood and the pain
gone in an instant
by what kind of magic?

Here in Jerusalem
thirty years later
the Romans besiege us,
an iron ring chokes us.

We fight for our food scraps,
snarling and cursing.
No dogs roam the alleys;
they have been eaten.
Doom is our future;
the Romans will kill us.
This is the end of us,
the end of our dreaming.
Where then is Yahweh
who promised to save us?
I've given up hoping.
All these long decades,
slave of the High Priest,
where has it brought me?
To death from a Roman
who will grin as he stabs me.
If I could escape it,
they'd soon see my heels.
But beyond the high wall,
on all sides around us,
I see the Jew-laden crosses
of those who sought freedom.
The Roman troops skewered them.
Doomed is our people,
nothing's more certain.
Die and be done with it,
that's what remains for us.
All these long decades
serving the High Priest,
and what has it got me?
Hawk-nosed old Caiaphas,
he was the worst of them;
slaves were like dirt to him.

I did what he ordered me,
but hated him, doing it.
That one was a schemer
behind his bland smiling,
behind his smooth talking;
his death brought rejoicing.

How well I remember,
one night at Passover
he took me with him
with a strong cohort —
the place was Gethsemane —
to capture a prisoner,
whose name was Jesus.
I heard them discuss it.
Troublemaker, they called him,
a threat to the nation.
I had no opinion,
it didn't concern me;
still, I was curious.
One of his followers,
a fellow named Judas,
came to the Temple.
Caiaphas bribed him,
I saw him do it.

We went to the Garden.
Judas was with us
and pointed out Jesus.
There in the torchlight
and shifting shadows
a giant leaped forward,
his sword held above him,

and flashing toward me.
I screamed with the pain of it,
the blood spurting freely,
then suddenly quiet.
Jesus called sharply,
"Peter, be patient!"
The soldiers fell backward.
Someone then touched me —
it was Jesus, they told me —
his touch brought my ear back,
I couldn't believe it.
Then his face came before me,
his eyes seemed to hold me.
I almost said,
"Yes, Lord,"
not knowing the reason —
something about him . . . .
But fear kept me silent,
fear they might
laugh at me
with Caiaphas watching,
smiling so coldly.
I ran into darkness,
among the deep shadows.

That night in the Garden,
how would it have changed things
if Yes was my answer?
Why does that moment
keep haunting my memory?
Jesus died on his gibbet,
as a criminal should die.
Why can't I forget it?

My fate is determined;
tomorrow will find me
slashed and then gutted
on the sword of a Roman.
Then I'll be finished . . .
is it really the finish?

I had my great moment;
why did I refuse it
that night in the Garden?
God, if you're listening,
help this poor servant.
The best I can offer
is the chill of my fearing.
That night in the Garden,
so many years distant,
I could have had loving,
I could have had warming,
my moment neglected.
God, if you hear me,
help this poor slave,
help this poor Malchus.

9

John Mark: A Headstrong Young Man

(Learning to Adapt)

Barnabas wanted to take along John,
called Mark. But Paul insisted that,
as he had deserted them at Pamphylia,
refusing to join them on that mission,
he was not fit to be taken along now.
The disagreement which ensued was so
sharp that the two separated.

Acts 15:37-39

Get Mark and bring
him with you, for he can
be of great service to me.

2 Timothy 4:11

A place on the road to Jericho

Paul was not so easy to get on with,
I'll say it now,
even in my old age,
when quarrels of the past should be forgotten.
Why should I rake over the burnt embers?
But since you asked about those days in Cyprus
I'll try to jog my memory.
I was a headstrong young man,
who chose to follow Christ,
and yet remained
a headstrong young man,
freely I, John Mark, confess it.

My mother was a follower of the Lord.

67

She heard him speak,
and saw him cure the sick,
and from that moment nothing shook her faith.
Some women stood and watched on Calvary
when Jesus died;
my mother was among them.
And in Gethsemane I myself was there
that night of shame
and saw them capture Christ.
Two Temple guards who knew me held my arms,
but I was agile, and I slipped their grasp
and ran away, leaving my shirt behind.
My mother then was braver than her son.

After Christ's death my mother's house became
a gathering place for all his followers.
There Peter came when he escaped from jail.
Rhoda, the maid, refused to let him in,
excited as she was and full of joy,
until he knocked again with louder blows.
What joy to hear the wonders of the Lord
from Peter as he told of his release!
And yet we knew our time of trial was near,
and some would be imprisoned, others die.
Preaching the name of Jesus was a crime.
The Sanhedrin had decreed that
even to speak his name was dangerous.
And so it was agreed that we should leave
Jerusalem and flee to other towns.
To Antioch is where I made my way,
and it was there I first heard "Christian" used
to signify a follower of Christ.
It was in Antioch I first met Paul,

fresh come from Tarsus,
breathing fiery zeal.
I was attracted to him, then repelled,
and then once more attracted. Such great zeal
and such an instinct to take charge of things!
If you were in his path he bowled you over.

When Barnabas and Paul conceived their plan
to preach the Gospel in Galatian towns,
they asked me to go with them.
I was young and eager.
It seemed venturesome,
and Barnabas was my uncle much admired.
We gathered on a Sabbath and our friends
invoked the Holy Spirit on our work
and sent us off upon our unknown roads
to all who longed to see the Savior come,
and thus we sailed for Cyprus.
There at first our mission prospered.
As a lively youth
I reveled in the journeys and the crowds
of natives that we spoke to.
Some there were
who contradicted Paul;
in Paphos, once
a court magician, Elymas by name,
opposed us bitterly
and was struck blind.
I saw it happen in the governor's house.
But Paul was restless, and he would not stay,
although it seemed the harvest was at hand.
"We must set out to sea again," Paul said.
"I want to visit Phrygia and beyond."

But Barnabas opposed him: "Here is work
to last us through the season."
I took sides with Barnabas.
We put it to a vote,
and Paul still had his way.
I didn't like it and told him so —
a youth will speak his mind.
Barnabas, a mild and gentle soul,
would not stand up to Paul, but on the ship
that brought us to the coast of Phrygia
I came to a decision in my mind.
And when we docked, I stayed upon the shore
and would not travel inland with the pair.
The vessel was returning soon to Syria,
and I was stubborn in returning home.

Paul took it hard, I know he did.
A few years later — wiser then
and more mature —I learned from Barnabas
another missionary trip was being planned.
He wanted me along, but Paul said No!
And nothing we could say
  would change his mind.
"I needed you in Lystra, Mark," he said,
"and yet you chose to leave me and go home."
Then Barnabas spoke up:
"Now, Brother Paul,
Mark is a good young man, and I insist
that he go with us on this arduous trip."
They argued back and forth, could not agree.
There were sharp words between them
and at last,
these two old friends each went his separate way.

I felt it keenly, having been the cause
of such great strife between these two good men.

Well, that's my story, now the years have passed.
But I have a pleasant sequel to relate:
Paul grew more gentle,
so, in truth, did I.
We met in Corinth and were reconciled.
I think Paul came to like me, in his way;
he shared his burdens with me willingly;
his age, my youth, both learned to live in peace.

When he was jailed in Rome he sent for me
to come and bring his books and heavy cloak
against the coldness of the winter there,
against the boredom of his house arrest.
Alas, I did not get to Rome in time
before he died along the Appian Way,
under a Roman sword.
Upon a cross,
Peter, my mentor, died on that same day.
But when Paul knew that death was close at hand,
he left with Luke some words to lift my soul:
"Tell Mark I'm sorry that I was so rude;
I've learned some lessons in my stormy life.
Three things are needed, faith and hope and love,
but love seems most important in the end.
Tell Mark I love him
in the love of God."

10

Magdalene: Lament and Song

(Love Responds to Love)

Jesus arose from the dead early on the first day of the week. He first appeared to Mary Magdalene, out of whom he had cast seven demons.

Mark 16:9

A panoramic view of the village of Nazareth

Lord, I proclaim your greatness,
My soul overflows with your love.
    They said of me in pity,
    "The devil holds her fast."
    I only knew that peace and love
    were memories of the past.
    My demons made me bitter,
    hate was my daily bread.
    I sneered at truth and goodness:
    "It's all a lie," I said.
    "No man on earth is honest;
    I'll trust them when they're dead."

Lord, I proclaim your greatness,
My soul overflows with your love.

> But when they dragged a woman
> out on the city street,
> and said she was a sinner
> and thrust her at your feet,
> their cruel eyes upon you,
> confident of their prize,
> you looked at her, Lord, with pity,
> and love was in your eyes.
> I watched you from a window,
> my heart leaped in surprise.

Lord, I proclaim your greatness,
My soul overflows with your love.

> Your way, Lord, was so gentle,
> your charity so pure,
> I knew within an instant
> I also could be sure
> you could command my demons
> and take away my sin.
> You had the power to do it,
> to still the selfish din
> within my soul and senses.
> I said: I will begin.

Lord, I proclaim your greatness,
My soul overflows with your love.

> I sought you out and found you
> there in a noisy crowd.

The Pharisees were scornful:
"Is this to be allowed,"
they said, "that such a woman
should kiss the Master's feet?"
I paid no heed to hypocrites.
I wept for joy to meet
the kindness that you showed me,
your healing words so sweet.

Lord, I proclaim your greatness,
My soul overflows with your love.

I wept in joyful freedom
from chains that bound my life,
with all the sordid moments,
the bitterness and strife,
the seven cruel demons
within and at my side.
Your love, Lord, has redeemed me
and saved me from my pride.
You gave me strength and courage
in Calvary's dark hour
to share the tortured moments,
to mourn your fading power.

Lord, I proclaim your greatness,
My soul overflows with your love.

What joy on Easter morning
to find you risen and free
from death. There in the garden
your glorious face to see,
and hear your greeting,

"Mary!" What joy it was to me.
Lord, I long for your coming,
but I am content to wait,
and if this Magdalene's story
of one who was blind and lame
frees others from their demons
and lifts them from their shame
to a love that is true and lasting,
that is sufficient fame.
Blessed, Lord, be your name.

Lord, I proclaim your greatness,
My soul overflows with your love.

11

Joseph Barsabbas: An Ordinary Man

(Need for Followers)

*They nominated two, Joseph
(called Barsabbas, also known as
Justus) and Matthias. Then they
prayed: "O Lord, you read the
hearts of men. Make known to us
which of these two you choose for
this apostolic ministry, replacing
Judas, who deserted the cause and
went the way he was destined to go."
Then they drew lots between the two
men. The choice fell to Matthias,
who was added to the eleven apostles.*

Acts 1:23-26

Scale model of the Temple in Jerusalem

I am no leader, nor an active type;
I have to think things out before I act.
Joseph the Just they call me. I suppose
it means that they admire my silent ways,
my unobtrusive keeping of the law.
But that was nothing great;
it was a case
of finding comfort in the proven ways
of Jewish law.
There's no way to explain
how Jesus came and turned my life around.
I met him at a wedding feast in Cana,
and he impressed me —
something about his eyes . . . .

But I was never one to leap ahead;
I'd rather wait and see how things work out.
I heard him preach
and saw him cure the sick,
and heard him tell the Pharisees their sins.
That made me fearful.
When on that day
he multiplied some loaves of bread, some fish,
and fed great crowds,
my mind came clear.
It was another kind of food I sought;
the bread of truth is what he offered me,
and with the truth
he bound my quiet heart
until the very end.

In Pilate's court I saw them bring him forth,
torn by the whips, and thorns upon his head,
a crown to mock his claim to be a king.
My anger rose, but still I did not speak
to those around me howling for his death.
I am no hero, but I am ashamed
I did not raise my voice in that dark hour,
or when they made him bear the heavy cross
upon his back and out to Calvary.
He fell along the way;
they seized a man
to help him with the cross, Simon his name.
He and his two sons — I know them well —
still serve Christ with all their hearts.

I saw the cross raised up on Calvary.
I saw it all, and thought the world would end.

Withered our hopes, we yet could not forget
his gentle words, the way he looked at us
with love and with compassion in his eyes.
We struggled with our misery and our fear.
And yet within a day of that event
there were strange rumors of an empty tomb.
We scarcely could believe them. With a friend,
Clopas by name, I walked to Emmaus,
a few miles distant from Jerusalem.
We were discussing yesterday's events
when someone joined us as we walked along.
He showed us how the prophets had foretold
all that had come to pass.
His words brought hope.
And when we both invited him to stop
at a wayside inn to sup with us,
he smiled and gave consent,
and there that night
we knew him
in the breaking of the bread.
This was the Savior, what abounding joy!
But even as we gazed at him in awe,
he vanished from our sight.

We hurried back
to tell what we had seen to his close friends —
Peter and John and Andrew and the rest.
Some of them had also seen the Lord,
but some had not, and they would not believe.
We had been sick with darkness and despair,
and such sickness takes a little time to cure.
But praise to God,
our hope has been restored,

and Christ our Savior, risen from the grave,
has shown his wounds.
To Thomas he said:
"Put in my side your hand and you will see
my wound is real, and I am truly Christ;
but blessed are those who will come after you
who do not see,
and yet their faith stays firm."

I am no preacher, no such gift have I,
and so I was surprised one Sabbath morn
when Peter spoke to all of us and said:
"Someone is needed who will serve the Lord
in place of Judas, now a suicide."
My name was one of those that Peter gave
as one who from the start had known the Lord.
Matthias was the other, and before
I could protest, it was at once arranged.
We would draw straws
  to see who would be called,
and so we did.
Matthias was the choice
and I was glad. I'm not the leader type,
I'm just a common ordinary man.
I know the gifts I lack; let others lead,
and I will follow in my quiet way.
Matthias is a good man, that I know,
not afraid to show authority
which is what apostles have to do,
and that is what I cannot do so well.

Now here it is a decade since that day
and brave must be the followers of Christ.

We can no longer openly profess
the name of Jesus;
those who do are jailed.
Some have died, like Stephen, who spoke out
against the executioners of Christ,
and so himself was executed too;
they crushed his head with stones,
even as he prayed:
"May God forgive them what they do today."

What will our future hold?
No man can tell.
Perhaps the world is coming to an end,
for many think that they can see the signs.
But no one really knows about these things,
the world may have 2,000 years to run.
I am content to leave it in God's hands;
my trust is in the ever living God.

12

Lydia: Dealer in Purple

(Openness to God's Word)

*We went to Philippi, a leading
city in the district of Macedonia,
and a Roman colony. We spent some
time in that city. Once, on the
Sabbath, we went outside the city
to the bank of a river, where we
thought there would be a place of
prayer. We sat down and spoke to
the women who were gathered there.
One who listened was a woman named
Lydia, a dealer in purple goods
from the town of Thyatira. She
already reverenced God, and the
Lord opened her heart to accept
what Paul was saying.*

Acts 16:12-15

A view of the Jordan River

Paul is dead,
dead by the sword in Rome —
that was the heart-stopping news
brought to us by a traveler from the West.
We had great hopes that he would be released;
although a prisoner, he could see his friends.
He wrote that he would meet us in Philippi.
Luke thought as much, and Timothy as well.
But Rome caught fire, and much of it destroyed
and many people burned. The emperor,
Nero was his name, had to blame someone,
so he blamed the Christians.
Paul and Peter died with many more,
herded like sheep into the slaughter house.

Peter on his common criminal's cross,
but Paul by the sword,
equally dead, but dead with dignity —
a Roman citizen deserves no less.
God help us
   when men play this game with death!
I weep for Paul, my father in the faith.

Here in my home
my work has lost its taste.
Always the purple dye could give delight.
I loved the boiling richness in the vats,
and when it cooled,
the depth of purple calm.
My husband taught me all his dyeing skills,
and he was skilled indeed in all he did.
The time was all too short —
one day he died,
killed in a foolish quarrel with a friend
over a trivial matter.
Men can be so senseless in these things.
I grieved for him, but I am not a person
to face the past; the future interests me.
I had no children,
work became my life.
I dealt with merchants
and with caravans,
coming and going on the Egnatian Way
to Rome and Athens and from Syria.
My dyes were in demand, I mixed them well.
I knew my business and they called me shrewd;
but I was fair, and though I bargained hard,
they saw that I was honest, and they knew

that if they tried to cheat me they would pay.
In Rome, I heard, my purple was the rage.
The senators all sought it for their robes,
and for their languid, fashionable wives.

But with success I knew my debt to God,
something within me reached out for the light.
I, a Gentile, had some Jewish friends,
and learned from them to keep the Sabbath rest.
Close to Philippi was a grassy place
along a tranquil river's mossy bank.
There with my household on the Sabbath day
I praised a God I really did not know
until one blessed morn
Paul came upon us and began to speak.
No tall, imposing preacher was this man —
squat, and with something of a stutter too,
but what great words
came tumbling from his lips.
He opened up my mind and heart.
I knew at once
my patient search was at an end,
and Christ became my way, and truth, and life.
I could not hear enough about his deeds
from Paul,
  who on Damascus road had seen the Lord
and came to know
Christ died for all, not only for the Jews.
So Paul, the unrelenting foe of Christ,
became an apostle for the Gentile world.

When Paul was ready to depart with Luke

and others in his group,
I told them, "No!
My house is large, please stay with me.
There is so much for us to learn of Christ."
It was not easy to convince this restless man,
always eager for the open road.
But those who know me say I have a will
of iron for decisions of this kind.
It may be so;
this much is clear to me:
we needed Paul to make us one with Christ.
And so he came, and in my Gentile house
the saving water flowed and made us clean,
and brought us light for all our darkened ways.
We broke the bread
and Christ became our food,
and others joined.
It was a time of joy,
a joy that made us babble when we prayed
and shout our praises of the living God.
I think we pleased the restless heart of Paul.
We could not hold him, but he held us dear,
his first-born Christians of the Western world.
He wrote a letter brimming with his love.
I have it in my home.
We cherish it,
and read it when we meet to break the bread.
And we can almost hear the voice of Paul
and see him standing in that awkward way,
tumbling out his words, or rather,
tumbling his heart,
that heart of his so filled
with Christ he never could contain his love.

And with that love he won us, nothing more;
for "love alone remains," he used to say.

Now Paul is dead
and will his work endure?
I know it will, although the storms may come.
And I must do my part to make it grow
among the Greeks and others that we meet.
My business prospers and my purple goods
are in demand;
I'm thankful to the Lord
that I can help the poor as Paul has asked.
The words he wrote are ever in my mind:
"To live is Christ,
but dying is my gain,
and I desire to die and be with Christ."
Now Paul is dead.
I mourn for him but I am joyful too,
for he has won his crown.
I ask his prayers
for those of us who still have crowns to win.

AFTERTHOUGHT

Now I will praise these godly men,
our ancestors, each in his own time:
the abounding glory
 of the Most High's portion,
his own part, since the days of old . . . .
All these were glorious in their time,
each illustrious in his day.
Some of them have left behind a name
and men recount their praiseworthy deeds;
but of others there is no memory . . .
yet these also were godly men
whose virtues have not been forgotten . . .
their bodies are peacefully laid away
but their names live on and on.
At gatherings their wisdom is retold
and the assembly proclaims their praise.

Sirach 44:1-15

More Popular Titles from Liguori Publications

Bibles

Good News for Modern Man
New Testament

Approved Catholic edition of this best seller. Complete with such special features as maps, word list, index of persons, places, subjects. *664 pages, soft cover, 95¢.*

The New American Bible
Old and New Testaments

Popular St. Joseph Edition. Includes Bible Dictionary, Doctrinal Bible Index, and more than 100 maps and photographs. *1,468 pages, 6 3/8" x 9 1/4", soft cover, $5.50.*

Discovering the Bible
by Rev. John Tickle

This book offers a basic background on the Bible plus 8 simple keys for learning and praying with the Scriptures. Suitable for individual prayer, CCD classes, high school and adult religion courses. 112 pages, 8½" x 11" soft cover, $2.95.

Good News from Matthew
by Joseph Moore, C.S.C.

Each chapter takes a key passage from St. Matthew and holds it up to the light of today's push-button world. The result is a new insight into Gospel words written so long ago. A book to help you relax, reflect and absorb the GOOD NEWS. 96 pages, soft cover, $1.95.

Children's Books

Growing Up With Jesus
by Francine O'Connor,
Illustrated by Kathryn Boswell

An activity/story book that lets children be creative while they learn about Jesus. Activities range from making original drawings to color-ins and finding hidden objects in pictures. The story progresses from the angel's visit to Mary through Jesus' birth and childhood to Jesus' work in the Church today. For ages 3 through 6. *32 pages, 8 ½" x 11", booklet, $1.00.*

A Catholic Child's Library

Includes four 45-page books. Mass Prayers for Children, Bible Prayers for Children, Old Testament for Children, and The New Testament for Children. *Set of four books $4.50.*

A Child's Story of Jesus

Includes three 45-page books. The Life of Jesus for Children. The Miracles of Jesus for Children, and The Friends of Jesus for Children. *Set of three books $3.50.*

Jesus Our Brother/*Revised edition*
by Francis and Anne Schraff

Complete, illustrated story of the life of Christ, written in simple language. Inspires youngsters to know more about

Christ and try harder to be like him. Great for short bedtime stories or for youngsters to read to themselves. Includes 20 playlets for children to act out. *160 pages, $1.95.*

Personal Growth

Three books by Ronda Chervin, Ph.D.

Love and Your Everyday Life
Helps you strive for perfect love of God in everyday life. 64 pages, 5⅛" x 7⅜", booklet, $1.00.

Prayer and Your Everyday Life
Helps you develop a personal relationship with God. 64 pages, 5⅛" x 7⅜", booklet, $1.00.

The Spirit and Your Everyday Life
You can fill your everyday actions and conversations with faith, hope, and love if you call on the graces of the Holy Spirit to help you. 64 pages, 5⅛" x 7⅜", booklet, $1.00.

Order from your local bookstore or send your order to Liguori Publications, Book Department, One Liguori Drive, Liguori, Mo., 63057. Please include 40¢ for postage and handling.

THE **LIGUORIAN** MAGAZINE

published monthly by the Redemptorists